What People are Saying about
IT'S TIME TO STAND UP

"It's TIME to STAND UP" is a powerful and urgent call to action for Christians and patriots alike that has grown into a rallying cry for America. It urges us to pursue truth, faith, and excellence in a time when our values are under relentless attack. This book serves as a timely reminder, especially when an election approaches, that the fight for our nation's soul is not just a fleeting battle but a long-term commitment. A must-read for those who believe in the enduring strength of Christian principles and the power of standing up for what is right.

~ ***Riley Gaines*** *12x NCAA All-American Swimmer, Advocate, Author*

Mickey's simple and clear message in "It's Time to Stand Up" is a "can't put down" commentary of the state of our nation today. He takes the two ideas of excellence and truth, two things that should be as clear as a bell to everyone, but as he says, "Unfortunately, what is convincing is too often believed over the truth." He makes the truth that we need to stand up for very convincing.

~ ***Reverend Thomas Koys***, *Pastor, Author, Pro-Life Advocate, Radio Show Host*

Occasionally a book comes along that is a must-read and IT'S TIME to STAND UP is one of them! In it my old friend, Mickey Straub, injects some optimism into this battle we are in to save the soul of our nation, and to prevent the transforming of America into just another European socialist state with unfettered government intervention and intrusion. I may be Australian born but I am a naturalized American citizen and embody the American spirit and passion. It is more important than ever today to stand up and work together to reverse the trends Mickey outlines in his new book.

~ *Nick Adams - Best-selling Author, Presidential Appointee, Founder, Foundation for Liberty & American Greatness (FLAG)*

In IT'S TIME to STAND UP, Mickey Straub is very direct about the need to restore truth and excellence in America and about the many similarities between the goals of the Democrats, Socialists, and the Communist Party USA, as well as the consequences. This is a timely message that needs to be told and read by every American. We need more bold biblical men of God to make themselves available to be used for God's purposes, and to do what is right in God's eyes for the advancement of God's kingdom...and that's why I highly recommend this book!

~ *Toni Stockton, Wife, mother of four, Homeschool Educator, Advocate, Writer, follower of Jesus*

I wholeheartedly endorse Mickey Straub's book IT'S TIME TO STAND UP! It's a Christian, patriotic book warning of the slippery slope we are heading in. No one could have convinced me that we would today be in the throes of an antisemitic culture. Christianity is next. Wake up America!

~ *Joe Jordan, Bestselling Author, Speaker, Icon, Corporate Trainer*

The timing of Mickey Straub's book, "It's Time to Stand Up...The Pursuit of Truth and Excellence in America," could not be better. Our Nation's citizenry is confused, disillusioned, and influenced by politicians, media, the mega-wealthy, and special interest groups that have deteriorated the very core and fiber of our great Country. One need not have to research for long to reach the conclusion, as Mickey aptly pointed out, that the state of our Country and its erosion of family values, faith, and education (especially in the poor and dependent communities) are not an accident.

~ *Richard Panico, Entrepreneur and Follower of Christ*

It's Time to Stand Up is a needed call-to-action that we need to end this era of cancel culture that has kept all of us silent for far too long. Mickey Straub's book reminds us that our democracy is based on conservative, Christian-based values and each of us has the power to keep the flame of American liberty alive.

~ *Suzanne Carawan, Marketing Executive, Author, Wife, and Mother*

"It's Time to Stand Up" is a powerful call to action for those who hold dear their faith and love for their country. This book brilliantly intertwines patriotic ideals with profound Christian principles, urging readers to rise up in defense of their beliefs and values. The compelling narratives and insightful reflections inspire a sense of courage and duty, reminding us that our voices and actions can make a real impact. A must-read for anyone seeking to strengthen their resolve in today's challenging times! It is time to stand UP!"

~ *Kathleen Hawkins*, *Business Advocate, Visionary, Speaker, Author*

In Romans 13:1-7, the Bible describes our responsibility and our relationship as Christian leaders with our nation's government. I pray that by reading Mickey's book you strive daily to align your thoughts and actions, as a citizen of our great nation, with God's will for your life. May Mickey's words stir your heart to action and that you take a stand for truth and excellence in the communities God has called you to serve.

~ *John D. Richardson*, *Leader of Leaders in financial services and several non-profit organizations*

This book provides insight and research I have never read, giving clearer understanding of historical expectations for our nation. It also gives us a challenge: Live up to those expectations now, at a time when our nation is making communal decisions on so many issues that will decide our fate.

~ *Mayor Jamie Clary*, *City of Hendersonville, Tennessee*

IT'S TIME to TIME STAND UP

The Pursuit of Truth and Excellence in America

MICKEY STRAUB

RL

It's Time to Stand Up

Cover design: Tamara Dever and Chastity Vasco
Editing: Karen Steinmann

Published by:
Roaring Lambs Publishing
17110 Dallas Parkway, Suite 260
Dallas, TX 75248

Published in the United States of America.

Dedication

It is tough to stand up. It is easier to appease, to avoid conflict and want to make people happy, and to focus on the easy and what brings us the most amount of pleasure now. But once the now passes, the future is here and it's a reflection of all we have done in the past.

America is what it is today because of the actions of those who came before us and upon whose shoulders we stand. We owe it to them to continue pursuing perfection no matter how futile, and to strive to preserve the foundation upon which our great nation stands.

We are at a pivotal time in history and, like Abraham Lincoln proposed to us over one hundred and fifty years ago, we have a choice and an opportunity to "highly resolve that these dead shall not have died in vain". This book is dedicated to America, God's country, and all those who fought this battle for truth and excellence before us and to all those who carry that mantle

Mickey Straub

forward.

Table of Contents

Preface

It's Time to STAND UP 10

Chapter 1

Pursuing Excellence 13

Chapter 2

Excellence Defined..........................21

Chapter 3

Seeking Truth..29

Chapter 4

The Decline of Excellence and Truth 33

Chapter 5

My Problem with Covid 45

Chapter 6

The Power of Prayer..55

Chapter 7

Getting Mad..61

Chapter 8

The Spreading of New Socialism..................65

Chapter 9

Consequences and Coincidences....................77

Chapter 10

Through the Eyes of Immigrants...................93

Chapter 11
    How to STAND UP..107
Chapter 12
    A Real-life Story...115
Chapter 13
    God's Call to Excellence 121
Acknowledgments 127
    About the Author...131
    About the Contributing Author.......................136

Preface
It's Time to STAND UP

The pursuit of Truth & Excellence in America

When my dear friend, fellow patriot, and brother in Christ, Glen Aubrey, asked me to join his inner circle of accomplished authors and friends, to write a chapter about thinking and being "Excellent," for his book, *Whatever is True*, I had a myriad of reasons not to do it. My excuses ranged from "I have too many other priorities and don't have enough time" to "I am not good enough or worthy."

Who knew that it would come to fruition at all, let alone be rewritten, rearranged, added to and retitled to become a book of its own and perhaps even a rallying cry for Americans? I suspect we all know the answer to that question.

As I resisted, and Glen persisted, I had this

gnawing feeling that God wanted me to do this. Another realization hit me, too, that, though my business might be about pursuing excellence and becoming your best, there have been too many times in my life that I have not been following my own advice.

Well, you can see how well my plan worked out for me. My love for truth and excellence, as well as for God and country, would eventually win out. As the saying goes, "When we make plans, God laughs".

May this book be a "Rallying Cry" for America, America's future, and the American people, to stand up for truth and excellence, as well as common sense. Remember, this is a marathon, not a sprint.

It's time to STAND UP,

Mickey Straub

Businessman/Mayor Emeritus/Author/
Patriot/Congressional Record Recipient

It's Time to Stand Up

Mickey Straub

Chapter 1
Pursuing Excellence

All of us must think differently than we often tend to do in our pursuit of excellence and resist that negative self-talk that we all sometimes hear internally, as well as from society at large. My resistance to write that chapter initially was one such moment, but Paul's words that Glen captured from Philippians 4:8 (NIV) in the first few pages of his book *(Whatever Is True)* kept echoing in my ears:

> *Finally, brothers and sisters… Whatever is true, Whatever is noble, Whatever is right, Whatever is pure, Whatever is lovely, Whatever is admirable, If anything is excellent Or praiseworthy, Think about such things.*

Why did the Apostle Paul give us that advice or directive? Why did he tell us to think about whatever is true, noble, right, pure, admirable, excellent, and praiseworthy?

The first thing that came to my mind was a motivational recording that I heard as an early teenager, a timeless message that I have listened to countless times and that has made a huge impact in my life. It is called *The Strangest Secret* by Earl Nightingale, and it was the first Gold Record self-improvement audio tape of its kind.

What is the Strangest Secret with which he inspired millions of people? Simply put, it is this:

"We become what we think about."

According to Mr. Nightingale, it is strange because it is a well-known truism agreed upon by virtually all philosophers and wise men and women, yet it virtually remains a secret to most people. But it is also a well-known strategy that some people seeking to destroy the American Dream use on a daily basis, as they seek to instill negativity and spread non-truths and fear to implement their agenda.

I have seen the impact of this secret and how much it can impact someone's life even in my own family. Many years ago, a niece of mine was a troubled teenager who started hanging out with the wrong crowd after her parents got divorced. She dropped out of college, lost her license after getting two DUI's (Driving Under the Influence), did not have a job, was living in the basement of her mother's townhome, and got pregnant out of wedlock.

The first book she chose to read (and summarize) upon my suggestion (but much to my surprise) was *As A Man Thinketh*, by James Allen. It helped change her life by helping her think differently in her pursuit of excellence! In her first summary, she wrote, "Changing my thought process has also given me a

16

purpose in my life and the power to try to achieve it. Even if I fail, I will keep trying and won't give up until I have accomplished everything that I set out to achieve. This will help build my strength and my character to be the person I want to be. *As A Man Thinketh*, although not a very large book, has completely changed my thoughts and my character."

To make a long story short, she proactively took responsibility for her life, walked into a real estate office (instead of applying online) and got a job as a receptionist. She eventually became a real estate agent and a very successful sales representative in another industry earning more than she ever originally thought possible. (And more than her uncle, I might add.) On top of that, she raised two wonderful children on her own (in Catholic school), went back to church, reunited with a high school friend, fell in love, and they are happily married. This is just one example of the power of thinking differently.

One can only assume that Apostle Paul knew this secret when he told his followers to "Think about these things," and the impact doing so could have on one's life and society in general. Chances are he was exposed to the concept of "becoming what you think about", a topic that was even addressed in the Book of Proverbs about 700 years earlier:

Proverbs 23:7 (KJV):

For as he thinketh in his heart, so is he.

As a footnote, my guess is that Earl Nightingale's inspiring words were rooted in scripture, as are most of the motivational, self-improvement messages we hear today.

The Apostle Paul knew that we move in the direction of our most dominant thoughts so that by "thinking about such things" such as being excellent, we would eventually become it. (Liberals know this, too, and use it very effectively.) I suspect that Paul told us what to think for our own good because he knew the consequences and he chose those words because he wanted to also assist (and encourage) us in our pursuit of heaven.

Yes, Apostle Paul told us what to think but, in many ways, he was also telling us how to think. What a gift! He also knew something that I just learned more recently in a book called *Fast-Starting a Career of Consequence* by Fred Sievert, the former president of New York Life who retired and attended the Yale Divinity School. In it, Fred quoted Arthur Miller's interpretation of Matthew 16:27: "We will be held accountable for our giftedness." What a concept and motivator for us all to think about these things and to use all of our God-given gifts to the best of our ability... because we are going to be held accountable.

Mickey Straub

Miller's words also reminded me of a quote by pastor and author Rick Warren I read many years ago that—if and when we get to heaven—God will ask us two crucial things:

1. What did you do with My Son, Jesus Christ?
2. What did you do with My gifts?

When Glen asked me to write about excellence, he said, "I have chosen you to invite you to do this because you are excellent." While that was a nice thought and a welcome compliment. I resisted, but in the end, I decided to follow where I thought that God was leading me (which I have been trying to do for years) and share some things that I think (and hope) God wants more people to hear.

This is a far departure from my early days and I'm probably the least likely person that anyone (especially my old friends in college and while living in California) would ever think would be preaching my faith and scripture based on my antics and lifestyle as a teenager and young adult. The most accurate description that I can give you is that "For most of my life, I have been a bad Catholic, but I was a really good sinner."

Guilt was also a motivator because I wanted to be better at "practicing what I preach." But then again, as a Catholic Christian, "I am trained to feel guilty" as the joke goes. It worked.

Chapter 2
Excellence Defined

So, what does it mean to be "Excellent" and was the Apostle Paul referring to only our thoughts or our actions, too?

By definition, "Excellent" is an *adjective* meaning "very good of its kind; eminently good; first-class; superior." ~ Merriam-Webster

In addition, I found the following: "possessing outstanding quality or superior merit; remarkably good and extraordinary."

The opposites (or antonyms) of "Excellent" are equally descriptive, if not diametrically opposed: atrocious, awful, and lousy. But even less dramatic terms like "mediocre" should inspire most people of reason to want to aspire to be excellent in all aspects of their lives.

After all, who wants to be considered mediocre? Not me. That is certainly one of the last words that I would like to have included in my eulogy, and I trust the same goes for you.

Literally, Paul only referred to what we should "think." But his push for us toward excellence would have to include both, since "thinking is always a precursor to activity" and, as we have seen, can dramatically impact our activity and results, both good and bad.

James, another apostle, also helps us connect the dots. When he tells us that, while we are saved by faith, not deeds, he states assuredly that faith without works doesn't work.

James 2:17 (NIV):

> *In the same way faith by itself, if it is not accompanied by action, is dead.*

At a minimum, mediocrity is the enemy of excellence and, in our working for the Lord, mediocrity is never an option. When we consider excellence, by definition, we are not contemplating anything less in what we 'think and do' in all aspects of life. A pursuit of excellence is God's command. Our responsibility is to obey. This is an eternal principle from God, Himself.

Once again, "In our working for the Lord, mediocrity is never an option." God's will and desire for us is to be Christ-like and to have eternal life with Him in heaven. That must be our goal and is, after all, why Jesus died for us on the cross.

Was Paul referring to our work, personal or spiritual lives, or all of the above?

Here is some good news: Excellence does not mean perfection. God does not expect us to be perfect, which the Apostle Paul and the other saints knew from personal experience. They were all sinners. But God does expect us to pursue perfection and to be "excellent" in our efforts to be Christ-like in all aspects of our life as we pursue eternal life in heaven with Him.

Out of all Paul's directives, this one resonates with me most and reminds me of Lexus' marketing slogan: "The Relentless Pursuit of Perfection." It also inspires us to try our best to achieve the most and regret the least in this earthly life, and to do the best with God's gifts in our pursuit of heaven.

The pursuit of excellence in this chapter also has a lot to do with what I do for a living. In 1995, I founded a patriotic, faith-based company based on helping sales professionals become their best using a concept and strategy we named "Activity Management." Because activities produce results, and we control our activity (God willing) it empowers them to control and manage their activity to create better results.

And it is probably no coincidence that it has American and biblical roots by how it promotes freedom, personal responsibility and reminds us of Jesus words: "Whatsoever a man soweth, that shall he also reap." (Galatians 6:7, KJV) In shorter terms, we reap what we sow.

It all starts with how you think, and it applies to virtually all aspects of life, from counting steps and calories, to praying the rosary, and to every sport and profession.

There is such a profound need and a cry for excellence in our world, especially these days! At the time I started writing this book, America was, and is, still recovering from the deadly effects of the Covid 19 pandemic and shutdowns. And I'm not just applying this to the mortality rates.

One of the grave side effects of it all was the decline of excellence in the workforce, in both quality and quantity. Far too many workers are not performing their jobs excellently (mediocre at best), and many people are unwilling to work at all.

The latter got even worse when the federal government increased and extended the unemployment benefits and gave so many "handouts" that many people made more money if they stayed home instead of going to work. As always, a satisfied need is no longer motivating. Camouflaged as good intentions, it put the decline in excellence on warp speed.

This lack of excellence is evident both in the workplace and our places of worship, and I'm not sure which one was harder hit. With the majority of churches being either shuttered temporarily or permanently, it was as if it was all intended to put a wedge between man and God? And it worked. One can only hope this was all part of God's plan, and that it will reverse soon, and the world will be better off. But it has been painful to watch.

Luckily, it has had the opposite effect in some places, where it has ignited people's faith and church attendance. I do know of one church in the Chicago Archdiocese, St. James at Sag Bridge, that more than doubled in size since the shutdowns started, and there are many more of which I am unaware. And, hopefully, more faith-filled pastors will fill the pews and the old silent majority is still the majority ... and will start standing up.

It's Time to Stand Up

Chapter 3

> **What did you do with My Son, Jesus Christ?**
> **What did you do with My gifts?**

Seeking Truth

Those are two great questions and worth repeating because they both lead back to our pursuit of excellence, to "think about such things" and, ultimately, to become them. They also remind us of "Why" we should do it, which fuels our fire to take action.

Though, in the end, the "What" is probably as equally important as the "How."

So how do we become "Excellent" in our personal, professional, and spiritual endeavors? What are the best steps, tips, and keys? And is there a magic formula?

Far be it for me to claim that I have all the answers to these vital questions. I do not and would bet that there have been hundreds, if not thousands of books written on this subject by people far more educated, wiser, more accomplished, wealthier, and successful than I have been blessed to become.

But I would like to address the one thing upon which excellence is built that might get overlooked. It is the one principle or value upon which excellence is also measured. It is the one thing that I didn't even know was of so much importance to me until I read a book many years ago called *The Path*, by Laurie Beth Jones.

The subtitle of her book is "Creating Your Mission Statement for Work and Life" which gives you a good idea of its content and purpose. Though I do not recall the exact details about the exercise in her book, the question that was asked I interpreted as something like, "What principle or value is so important to you that you would go to your deathbed to prevent it from being eliminated from society?"

After reviewing the list of alternatives, the answer that I came up with was this: *truth*.

So, what does truth have to do with excellence? In a word, *everything!* The only way one's performance in any endeavor can be determined is if it is based on accuracy, i.e., truth.

Of course, things like desire, commitment, action, measurement are all needed, but the foundation of it all has to be truth.

Truth is the first prerequisite. Without accuracy, there can be no truth. Without truth, there can be no excellence. Without measurement, there can be no accuracy. Without desire, there will be no effort (action).

One of my dear friends, Padraic O'Connor (a carpenter from Ireland who I met at that church I mentioned) put it best in a recent conversation when he said,

"You cannot be excellent without embracing the truth. They are not separate issues; you can't have one without the other. Truth is a destination. Excellence is the journey; it's where you make changes and become better people: by embracing the truth."

He also added: "Confusion (of truth) is one of the tools that Satan uses to destroy society."

I couldn't agree with him more in all aspects of life! We need to have a standard on which we compare ourselves and it has to be based on *truth*.

Chapter 4

The Decline of Excellence and Truth

Whatever is True was a fitting title for Glen Aubrey's last book since truth applies to all of its precepts, especially when it comes to being "Excellent." With "excellence and truth" being such important principles in my life, you can imagine how difficult it has been for me to watch what has been happening in America over the last few years.

In your lifetime, did you ever think that you'd see such a decline of truth and excellence in our society? For example:

Did you think that your government would:

1. Confine you to your home?
2. Prevent you from being able to see sickly loved ones in hospitals or

nursing homes?

3. Stop you from attending church or receiving communion?

Did you ever think:

1. We would see our national monuments being destroyed or protesters be allowed to freely loot businesses, injure at will, or attack police officers, and do it without consequence or punishment?

2. Politicians could get away with telling lies about their opponents with no proof or accountability or professional athletes disrespecting the America Flag?

3. That spiritual tepidity (lukewarmness) would be so widespread in America that belief in God and heaven would wane, people would stop practicing their faith, and the rabid increase of atheists?

Mickey Straub

Would you ever expect that in America, a federal agency that oversaw disease control could:

1. Decide if your job was essential or non-essential?
2. Force you to wear a face mask that was as effective at preventing a virus from spreading as a chain link fence would be to keep out mosquitos?
3. Mandate you to get an experimental drug, they called a vaccine, that did not actually vaccinate you from getting infected by the disease it was targeting?
4. Then make it financially attractive (legally) for all medical facilities to attribute virtually all of the deaths to the new virus (Covid 19) and none to the old one (Influenza) even though the symptoms were the same, as long as they tested positive, even if it was the result of a drowning?

Unfortunately, the decline in truthfulness in America has been increasing at what feels like Mach 1 speed in recent years. These days, if a man puts on a dress, some Americans want you to believe that he's a woman. That's a lie, defies common sense, and it is an assault on God, man's creator. It is also an attempt to push God out of our lives, which they are doing very well.

There is a group in America that is turning truth upside down to distract people. I saw this firsthand while the mayor of a prominent Chicago suburb and during my visits to the state capitol; when the politicians on one side of the aisle (mostly) would repeat a lie so often that some people would accept it as the truth no matter how blatantly false it was or how it defied common sense.

Did you ever think that well-intentioned, liberal citizens would:

1. Believe and push that there are more than two (2) genders in the human race, let alone seventy-two (72) more, which they now claim? God created two (2) genders: male and female. (Hello … He created Adam and Eve, not Adam and Steve!)

2. Encourage and openly promote homosexuality and gay marriage on television, in parades, schools and in the movies in the name of equality but to the detriment of the family?

3. Indoctrinate our kids, and force adults, to use pronouns?

4. Did you ever think that our schools would be allowed to teach third graders about homosexuality and explain how it is performed?

5. What about some prominent high schools, which I knew of in an upscale Chicago suburb, whose administrators allowed "Furries" (students dressed up

as animals) and would succumb to even putting cat litter boxes in the restrooms?

Truth is now subjective, at least that's what liberals want you to think. Here is their modus operandi — Deny, Distort, and Distract — and the name of the one responsible begins with the same letter, the "Devil." I guess that shouldn't surprise us since, as Jesus told the Jews in John 8:44 (NIV):

"When he (Satan) lies, he speaks his native language, for he is a liar and the father of lies."

Did you ever think you would see the day when the integrity of our (coveted) democratic elections would be called into question?

Did you ever think that public schools would ever allow boys to compete in girls' sports, or put sanitary napkins in the boys' bathrooms, or allow boys to have access to girls' bathrooms? The latter was confirmed by a friend in Chicago, a successful restauranteur who asked her shapely sixteen-year-old female employee why she was dressing so promiscuously? She told her that the same boys who play for the football team on the weekend come into school on Monday and claim "Gender Dysphoria," i.e., they "identify" as a girl that day, so they can access the girls' room to have sex with a willing partner.

She wants to be one of them. (I'm not making this stuff up … it's happening!)

Thank God that Roe vs. Wade was recently overturned by the U. S. Supreme Court, which, I hope, shows some promise that truth and excellence may be coming back in vogue!

Abortion is such a violation of both, and I hope that in the year 2122, people will look back and say, "Do you mean that Americans

100 years ago actually murdered millions of innocent defenseless babies under the guise of calling it a mother's "Choice", and claiming that a baby in a mother's womb was not considered to be a human being?" What about the baby's choice? God's choice?

The left has been so good at their marketing and messaging that some people believe it's a choice, not a child. (So claims the supposed party of science.)

I once heard Dennis Prager, conservative talk show host and author at a dinner event, say that what he likes to ask liberals is this: "If it's not a human being, then what is it? Is it a zygote? A pimple?" Crickets. That's all he could hear. I have often wondered, "Why do liberals only point to "Science" when it fits their narrative and agenda? Well, I guess we all know the answer to that one.

"Claiming there are more than two

genders" is another ridiculous and indefensible position when it comes to science or common sense. Bluntly put, it's an outright lie and the same goes for anyone claiming they can change their gender because of how they "feel," whether it's for a day, month, year, or a lifetime. Just because I wake up "feeling like an Astronaut" doesn't mean that I can fly to the moon!

Excellence and truth are synonymous, and there is a profound need for more of both in today's world! Did you ever think that you would hear so many half-truths, non-truths, twisted truths, and outright lies so pervasively being spread in our society by even government officials, federal agencies, and media outlets?

Where is the higher standard today?

This is the devil's handiwork, and we would all do well to remind ourselves of how

Reverend Anthony J. Paone, S. J. put it in his book called *My Daily Bread*. He described the devil as "The enemy of Truth" and Jesus as "The Author of Truth."

Unfortunately, liberals and the liberal media have taken lying to an art form, much like the Naziism and Communism did in the 1940s. The Russians, though, took that to a whole new level in their goal to influence and control its citizens through the media. In 1912, the official newspaper of the Central Committee of the Communist Party of the Soviet Union was formed called PRAVDA, which is Russian for "Truth." How is that for irony and creative marketing? (I first learned about Pravda from a political science professor while attending college; it was a way of camouflaging their lies and continues today.)

When our federal government's warnings about the Covid pandemic were first aired

43

through the mainstream media, they made it sound like people would be dying and melting in the streets if exposed to a passerby, it made me think of Pravda, and what I heard happened when Orson Welles' *War of the Worlds* radio drama that caused mass hysteria was aired live on October 30, 1938.

The episode was an adaptation of H.G. Wells's novel of the same name and was directed and narrated by Welles for the CBS Radio Network's "The Mercury Theatre on the Air". The episode included a regular music program, news bulletins and actors portraying reporters and government officials.

This radio broadcast is famous for inciting a panic by convincing some members of the radio listening audience that a Martian invasion was taking place and it was reported that it caused mass panic and people were jumping off balconies.

Though the scale of panic is disputed, just one life lost would have been tragic, but it demonstrated the power of the media and messaging from government officials, real or not. Why? Because we become what we think about. Instead of following Apostle Paul's advice to "think about such things" that are positive, they focused on negative things, fear and worldly possessions. And since they believed what they were hearing, they acted irrationally and made some fatal mistakes.

From the moment I heard the radio, television, and internet warnings about Covid that were predicting doom and death in the streets, I likened it to that Orson Welles' radio broadcast and questioned the accuracy of the exaggerated predictions and government solutions. Unfortunately, history has done little to dispel those suspicions, only reinforcing them.

Chapter 5
My Problem with Covid

I wasn't planning on relating my Covid experience, including an 11-day hospital stay in isolation on oxygen, but it seems only fitting when you put it to the truth, excellence and common-sense test. Were any of the early predictions of death and destruction accurate? Did masks really work, and did the pandemic really have to last almost three years? Were the mortality rates exaggerated when hospitals were being incentivized to blame Covid for being the cause?

My apologies ahead of time to anyone who thinks differently and/or who lost a loved one due to Covid or the physical infirmities it targeted, and anyone who believed everything the government told you. I'm sorry for your loss, but here is my story.

In early August of 2021, I started feeling sick with what I thought were flu symptoms. As usual, I tried to fight them off by improving my diet and sleep habits, but my condition continued to worsen. Finally, after several days of my wife telling me to get tested, I went into a Loyola medical facility and, sure enough, I tested positive for Covid.

Always the optimist, and reluctant to seek medical attention, I continued with over-the-counter medications and my own treatments, plus added a plethora of natural remedies, courtesy of a caring dear friend (Thank you, Sam Barakat!), but all unsuccessfully. After a few more days of a fever and worsening symptoms, my wife and I sat down for lunch at the kitchen table. It was then I realized that I just didn't have enough energy to even eat and finally gave in to having her drive me to the Palos Community Hospital, which was being bought out by Northwestern Medicine.

When I arrived at the Emergency Room, I was even weaker, and didn't have the energy to eat or fight and my energy level was so depleted that I didn't know if I would ever recover.

I had reached a point of accepting whatever outcome God had in store for me, just as Jesus had taught us to do in the Lord's Prayer from His Sermon on the Mount: "Thy will be done." It was a scary, but peaceful feeling.

Luckily, there were many of the old guard still working at the hospital, my wife's fellow co-workers, still working at the main hospital (that was originally Catholic) for which my wife, Charmaine, had worked as a Registered Nurse for over forty years. That was comforting and made my transition from freedom to isolation I was about to endure a lot easier. Though I never thought (should I recover) that I would not be allowed to see family or friends for longer than a few days, let alone for over a week!

Chest X-Rays showed that I had bilateral pneumonia and, as my wife had already confirmed, "my lungs, sounded like crackling glass." In addition, I was running a high fever and suffered from dehydration.

My team of doctors put me on IV fluids and 24/7 oxygen beginning at 2-3 liters. They then quickly raised it up to 11 liters for most of my stay. (I was told that this was the highest level allowed nasally, right below requiring a metal mask, then a ventilator.) I also took vitamins C, D, E, and Zinc daily, and they put me on a steroid called Decadron, plus infusions of Remdesivir, a drug with anti-viral benefits.

From my first day in the hospital, I asked about Hydroxychloroquine and Ivermectin, which was how President Donald Trump and many friends and acquaintances had been (successfully) treated for Covid. But three out of my four doctors kept telling me that they would not recommend it, that their medical society advised against it, and that it was not an option for me at that hospital.

I did not know, and was not told, that Remdesivir was also quite controversial and known to have serious, and even lethal, side effects, like kidney failure. One could argue that the use of both drugs was subjective, but truth and excellence were also called into question.

Having made little progress, on day five I agreed with my primary pulmonologist, Dr. Samran Haider, for me to start taking an experimental drug, Barcitinib, that was not approved by the FDA for Covid, though it was commonly used for rheumatoid arthritis and approved through an EUA (Emergency Use Authorization). I was told that Barcitinib was used for decreasing inflammation in the lungs and body but had the side effect of lowering the immune system. There was another drug, Actemra, that they wanted to use first, but there was a national shortage, and it was unavailable.

Up until day five, and for the first time in my life, I hadn't shaved, brushed my hair, or even really bathed. (The hospital staff did a great job overall, though my hygiene or bed sheets were not priorities for them.) After I changed my attitude (thinking differently), shaved, washed my hair and body, started to do light exercise daily, plus do breathing exercises (three sets, eight times a day) and remained prone (laying on my stomach) for 12-16 hours a day (doing differently) I started feeling better consistently, day by day and my guess is that treatment also played a role, as did my thinking differently. I was kept on 11 liters of oxygen, but my pulse oxygen level gradually improved a little daily.

Constantly, I told every doctor, nurse, nurse's aide, and even the staff delivering the food, about three things: how long my wife had worked there, how excited I was about my faith. and how much I appreciated what they were doing for me. (Besides all that being true, it pays dividends to have friends and to be nice! We reap what we sow.)

The other thing that I did was "Focus on Jesus" from Day One, and I prayed the Rosary every day! I had only brought two pieces of reading material with me when I scrambled to leave my home: a Knights of Columbus *Columbia Magazine* and a little book called, *What does Jesus mean to me?* (I had received the latter back in 2008 from a born-again Christian friend of mine, the late Charlie "Tremendous" Jones, and finally completed reading it during my stay.)

I also binged on Christian movies every night by watching every episode of Seasons One and Two of *The Chosen* (for the second time) and streamed *Pureflix* movies. I'll never forget the one line in one of their movies from a former Hell's Angel motorcycle guy turned Christian, who would ask perfect strangers, "Hey, do you know Jesus?"

The last thing I ever expected to do while in the hospital was to focus on Jesus for ten straight days, or to evangelize from my hospital bed, but that's exactly what I did.

Was it a miracle for me to leave the hospital after eleven days of receiving the maximum level of oxygen which can be administered nasally, with no restrictions and requiring only one prescription for baby aspirin?

I don't know. But what I do know is this: faith and thinking (plus doing) differently

53

were the turning points. I also believe, undoubtedly, that praying every day, focusing on Jesus, and having prayer groups of friends and family all over the country pray for my survival, was the difference maker. I also wouldn't doubt that praying the Rosary every day for the previous nine years (which included breathing exercises) helped prepare me for what I was to go through.

> "When air becomes the priority,
> everything changes."

During my last, post-hospital visit with one of my doctors, he was still adamant about me getting the Covid vaccine. He also continued to minimize the role of natural immunity, as did a brother of mine who said it was all my fault since I refused to get vaccinated.

So, I asked the doctor, "Does the vaccine guarantee that someone who takes this vaccine won't get Covid?" He said, "No." Next, I asked, "Does it guarantee that one taking the vaccine can't carry Covid?" Once again, he said, "No." Then, I asked, "Will the vaccine guarantee that I can't transmit Covid?" He said, "No."

So, then I asked him, "If the vaccine doesn't vaccinate, why would I ever want to get the vaccine?" The best answer he could give was this: "To minimize future symptoms and to avoid the side effects of the drugs they will give you to get over Covid."

After finding out that he had a daughter who was only a couple of years old, I asked him, "Are you going to get her vaccinated?" He said, "No." As I am sure you have already guessed, I chose the same answer for me, and discouraged vaccine use at my household.

Unfortunately, what is convincing is too often believed over the truth. That was one of my final lessons in public office and was certainly the case when it came to the pandemic.

Chapter 6

The Power of Prayer

Covid was a blessing and a curse to me. There were times that I was tempted to give up, but God had other plans. I even wrote about the pros and cons while in the hospital, then posted and shared this immediately

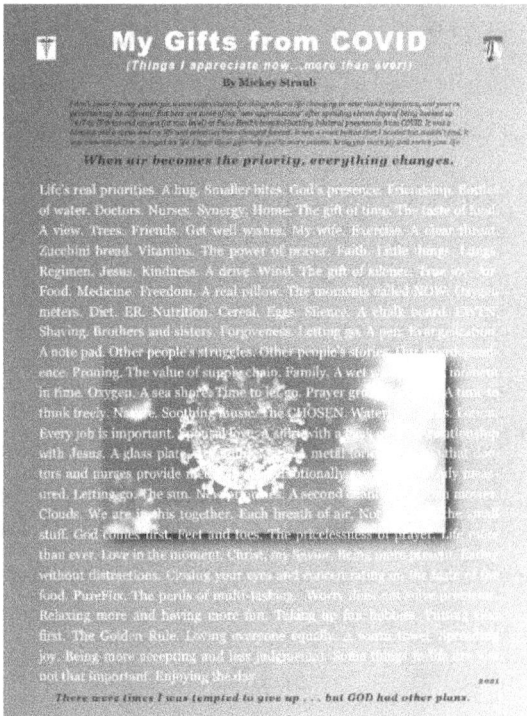

afterward…

There was also one more thing that happened while in the hospital that was so timely it was uncanny, serendipitous, and we think providential, that has to do with the picture on the next page.

Three days after I was admitted to the hospital, Charmaine, my wife, had been home recovering from her much milder case of Covid. She was distraught and worried about whether, or not, I would survive.

She decided to get out of the house, reasoning she wouldn't put anyone in harm's way if she took a drive in her convertible by herself, to get some fresh air.

Charmaine drove south on Route 83 and took a right at the Clark Gas Station toward the Waterfall Glen Forest Preserve. As she made the curve north toward the Argonne National

Laboratory property, she noticed the beautiful, bright blue sky ahead of her which reminded her of a picture (below) that I had taken of her

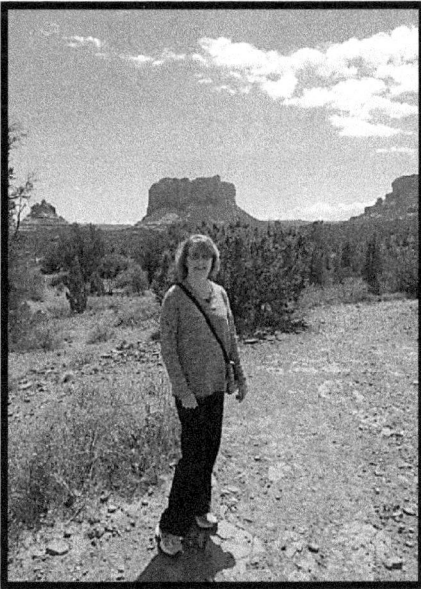

during a visit to Sedona, Arizona a few years earlier.

Charmaine Straub, Sedona Arizona

She decided to drive in its direction and,

along the way, thought to herself, "If Mickey gets through this, we'll have to go back there to visit."

Instead of heading toward home, she drove toward where the sky was bluest, making a left at the first light and pulled into the National Shrine of Saint Therese of Lisieux. Though it was located at Our Lady of Mt. Carmel in Darien, Illinois not far away, she never knew then it even existed.

She sat in the gazebo, prayed for my recovery, and cried. Then she stood in front of the statue of St. Teresa of Avila that she felt drawn to, prayed again, and took a walk around the grounds to see the many other statues. Along the way, she stopped and prayed to God that He would restore my health because my work here was not yet completed.

My wife drove home, pulled into the

garage, and went about her day. Then, a few hours later, her phone randomly dinged and, for no particular reason, up came the very same picture that I took of her in Sedona that she was thinking about when she was driving to the Shrine!

That was Charmaine's sign that her prayers (and everyone else's) were being heard. On that day, she thought to herself, "This is God's way of telling me Mickey is going to be okay." Her entire outlook changed, and it was the same day before my health turnaround began. That was one more reason why we should never underestimate

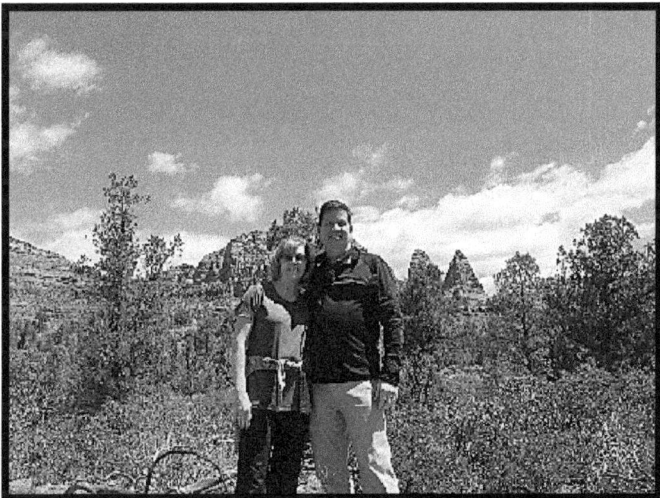

Mickey Straub

the power of prayer.

Charmaine and Mickey Straub,
Sedona, Arizona

It's Time to Stand Up

Chapter 7
Getting Mad

As I write this chapter and think of what we have seen change in recent years with societal norms, public education and the socialist policies being pushed and implemented by liberal politicians and in our schools, the near doubling of food prices and gasoline prices and 60% of Americans now living paycheck to paycheck and many in poverty, plus the highest inflation rate in 50 years—a scene in an old movie called *Network* comes to mind.

It is the scene, and memorable plea, of a News Anchor, Howard Beale (played by Peter Finch), while he's delivering the *Evening News*:

Speech from *Network* (1976 film)

"I don't have to tell you that things are

bad. Everybody knows things are bad. It's a Depression! Everybody's out of work or scared of losing their job. The dollar buys a nickel's worth. Banks are going bust. Shopkeepers are keeping guns under the counter. Punks are running wild in the street and there's nobody anywhere that seems to know what to do and there's no end to it.

"We sit watching our TVs while some local newscaster tells us that today we had 15 homicides and 63 violent crimes as if that's the way it's supposed to be. We know things are bad, worse than bad, they're crazy!

"It's like everything everywhere is going crazy so we don't go out anymore. We sit in the house and slowly our world we're living in gets smaller, and all we say is, 'Please, at least let us leave our living rooms? I won't say anything. Just leave us alone.' Well, I'm not going to leave you alone! I want you to get mad!

Mickey Straub

"I don't want you to protest, I don't want you to riot. I don't know what to do about the depression and the inflation and the Russians and the crime in the street. All I know is first you've got to get mad! So, I want you to get up now! I want all of you to get up out of your chairs, I want you to get up right now and go to the window, open it, and stick your head out and yell: 'I'm as mad as hell, and I'm not going to take this anymore!'

"Things have got to change. But first, you've got to get mad! Stick your head out your window and yell: 'I'm as mad as hell, and I'm not going to take this anymore!'"[1]

If a remake of that movie was produced today, I'm afraid the storyline wouldn't

---

[1] © Speech from *Network* (1976)
https://m.youtube.com/watch?v=ZwMVMbmQBug&pp=ygUNTmV0d29yayayBtb3ZpZZQ%3D%3D

change much; only the circumstances described would paint a much more dismal and bleaker picture, and with less chance of redemption, than the one Howard Beale described the night of his newscast.

You would think that we would have learned, but history has a way of repeating itself.

Chapter 8

The Spreading of New Socialism

(A Civil War, of sorts)

The public education system, our largest government monopoly that most closely resembles socialism, is an abject failure and America's international ranking has been declining for decades. Here is just one example, according to World Population Review: In 2005, the U.S. ranked 4th in math scores and 5th in science. But in 2018, just thirteen years later, the U.S. ranked 38th in math scores and 24th in science. This should concern all of us.

Before going any further, though, I think it's prudent that we all first get a better understanding of what socialism is and how it is defined. You're welcome to do what I did and just Google it. The definition is hiding in plain sight, and I hope is helpful to you as you assess the current state of affairs.

According to Webster's Dictionary, it is defined as follows:

Socialism [soh-sh*uh*-liz-*uh*m]
noun

1. a theory or system of social organization that advocates the ownership and control of the means of production and distribution, capital, land, etc., by the community as a whole, usually through a centralized government.
2. procedure or practice in accordance with this theory.
3. (in Marxist theory) the stage following capitalism in the transition of a society to communism, characterized by the

imperfect implementation of collectivist principles.

There are some who believe that what we are seeing today in America is not as bad as what the world saw flourish in Eastern Europe almost a hundred years ago. Instead, they rebrand it as a new form of Socialism because the government does not, in most cases, technically "own and control the means of production and distribution of products, capital and land." That and they may be technically correct in some cases, but what the government does do today is control those industries through taxation, over-regulation, and some form of compensation to control them, and the outcome is virtually identical.

Anyone can make wild claims with no evidence, then market it well and many people will believe it. But let me give you just one example that I personally experienced and saw in action that demonstrates how the government exerts control without ownership:

Several years ago, I noticed that the Christmas cards that I was receiving from a private liberal arts college, founded in 1855, no longer had any mention of Christmas on their annual cards to donors. This came as quite a surprise since it was founded by the Disciples of Christ Christian Church, so I asked the then college president why they were now called "Holiday Cards" with no mention of Christmas or Jesus' birth? He told me that, "The college needed to adhere to federal regulations like this or they would lose the federal scholarship money upon which they needed to survive."

That was quite a wake-up call for me, and an education on how government can control the private sector. What made this even more startling was that it was happening at President Ronald Reagan's alma mater, Eureka College, in Eureka, Illinois. This is a clear example of the New Socialism.

I can't explain all the reasons why this is happening or why I would get to know people on the inside who would share their stories with me. I can only assume that all these coincidences are all part of God's plan. And here's another one:

An older woman lived behind us that we didn't see much for most of the thirty-six years we lived in our previous home in Illinois. Most often, we could see her car driving away early in the morning and coming home late. A few years before she moved, we learned from Carol that she owned an academic book publishing company for fifty years that distributed across the schools in our nation. But what was disturbing to her most, and shocking to us, was when she told me:

"They have been dumbing-down our

schoolbooks for years!"

I have no idea why this has been happening, nor how to fix it or why the U.S. Department of Education would allow it to happen? I am just a messenger. But hopefully someone much smarter than I am in these areas will read this book and be inspired and guided to devise and execute a plan to reverse this atrocious and self-destructive trend in America?

There are other issues, too, that have not been handled well especially in those major cities run by liberal, career politicians, like the crises we face in mental health, suicide, drug addiction, crime rates and homelessness. These have all been further exacerbated in recent years by the federal government's open border policy that has allowed the influx of several million illegal immigration to cross our southern border freely.

What has been especially disturbing to my wife and me – and one of the reasons why we left Illinois – has been the flood of socialistic district attorneys who refuse to prosecute crimes that have led to a huge rise in violent crime. Chicago alone, which was just twenty miles away from our previous home, has seen the number of homicides skyrocket. The city recorded nearly 770 homicides in the first year of the pandemic, 2020, which was up 50% from the previous year! The *Chicago Tribune* even reported a couple of years ago that the city broke a 25-year record when it surpassed 800 homicides. That's over two per day…and one of the motivating reasons we moved to Tennessee! Those in charge try to blame it on systemic racism, but that defies common sense since 97% of homicides and shooters were black, as are virtually all of the Windy City's top government and political leaders.

The pandemic also revealed a stunningly

incompetent, socialized medical and health care system, which probably killed more people in nursing homes than it saved, while counting anyone who died as victims of Covid because they tested positive, even though they actually drowned or died in a motorcycle accident. And with all the fearmongering that the government has peddled, two years later many people are still too scared to go to social gatherings, to work, or drive a car alone, without wearing a mask, which drives me crazy! Some people still don't want to even leave their home, while others can still be seen driving their cars while wearing a mask.

If all that is not enough—when it comes to the lack of truth and excellence—to get every American mad, I don't know what is! But there is one possible explanation, and it is explained in this old story:

A guy was walking down the street and, when he was about to pass by an old man's house, he noticed there was a dog on his porch that was barking and howling, barking and howling. So, he asked, "Excuse me old man, but why is your dog barking and howling?" The man replied, "Well, it's because he's sitting on a nail." Perplexed, the guy asked, "But, why doesn't he get off the nail?" The old man said, "Because it doesn't hurt bad enough yet."

That must be it? As bad as it is, "It doesn't hurt bad enough yet."

Maybe the decline of truth and excellence — along with morals and freedoms — has happened so slowly that it doesn't hurt bad enough? Hopefully, now that more parents have learned how our educators are teaching our second-grade children about transgenderism and gender dysphoria, using sexually explicit photographs that would be considered pornographic if presented by a stranger at the library, plus the alleged "systemic racism" and anti-American propaganda that our public (and some private) schools are peddling, maybe that will finally be enough to get people mad?

Oh, how I wish that every American could have heard just a fraction of the warnings that I have heard from (legal) immigrants from Egypt, Kuwait, Croatia, Mexico, Russia, Poland, Cuba, China and many others, about how they are seeing things the very same things in America that caused them to leave their own countries. Here's one of the most glaring examples that got my attention and it happened at the barber shop last summer:

As I was sitting in the barber chair, unmasked per usual, I noticed a fully masked Asian man come in, sit down, and stare at me—at least that is what it felt like he was doing! Feeling a bit uncomfortable, and wanting to be sensitive to his concerns, I was almost out the door when I overheard him say something to the other barber about how crazy this pandemic was. So, I stopped and confirmed what I heard. Then he said something that I will never, ever forget...

"I moved here from China 30 years ago, and I have to tell you that America is looking more and more like China these days and, unless you white guys start standing up, we're screwed!"

That was not what I expected...especially coming from a Chinese guy!

There are many people who don't want to even talk about this subject, that America is moving toward Socialism, if not Fascism, usually followed by Communism, which many believe is already here. Or that our country is so divided. It is like we are in a subtle Civil War, albeit with no bullets, at least mostly. But there is plenty of evidence to suggest otherwise.

Andrew Jackson's quote comes to mind: "But you must remember, my fellow citizens, that eternal vigilance by the people is the price of liberty, and that you must pay the price if you wish to secure the blessing."

The reality is that we have not continued to pay the price, and the America we once knew, loved and was respected by the world is slipping away. We have not been vigilant.

Chapter 9

Consequences and Coincidences

It would be an unfinished book and I would be remiss if I didn't at least begin to address some of the consequences of our inaction and, "What types of things all of us can do to take action?"

What are the consequences of inaction, of not standing up? The short answer is more of the same of what we have seen in recent years, which is the growth of socialism, the decline of truth and excellence in government, the rise to power of more politicians who do not have America's founding principles and best interests at heart and the increased loss of our freedoms, liberty, and the American way of life as we know it. At worst, it could mean the gradual move toward Fascism, Marxism and/or Communism resulting in dissolution of the American Dream and the country as we know it. The risk is that that our children, grandchildren, great grandchildren and beyond will never be blessed to live in what we knew as the greatest country in the world and the beacon of hope for the rest of the world will perish.

Unfortunately, the political party that I grew up with and was born into, is not what it used to be and is on the wrong path. As a result of our inaction, as well as perhaps their desire for power, money and turning their back on truth, excellence and God in general, the Democratic Party is almost unrecognizable today. Neither of our major political parties are perfect, but President John F. Kennedy's old party and its priorities and socialist-like policies would be more accurately described as the Democratic Socialist Party, hence the reason why our public education and health care system have become what they are today.

There are some who even believe, with good reason, that it is the Democratic Communist Party camouflaged as Socialists.

One only needs to take a look at the agenda and priorities of the Communist Party USA (CPUSA.org) to see the resemblance to that of today's Democratic Party. Here is list of CPUSA's priorities from their actual website back in 2012 which are radical indeed:

The Communist Party USA was founded in 1919 in Chicago, Illinois

The Communist Party stands for the interests of the American working class and the American people.

- Organizations fighting for equality and social justice.
- The environmental movement.
- Immigrant's rights groups and the "Health Care for All" campaign.
- We work in coalition with the labor movement, the peace movement, and the student movement.

CPUSA also claims, "But to win a better life for working families, we believe that we must go further. We believe that the American people can replace capitalism with a system that puts people before profit — socialism. We are rooted in our country's revolutionary history and its struggles for democracy."

Do their priorities look familiar? If you think they sound like those of the current Democratic National Committee, you wouldn't be alone. Here is a quote from historian Ron Radosh to the BBC even back in 2014 about the Democratic Party:

> *"The positions they take are really indistinguishable from the left-wing social democratic groups."*

Even their protest signs closely resemble the Democratic Party's marketing message and campaign strategy today, sound bites that sound appealing but are disingenuous like: "Protect Our Democracy."

From what we all have been seeing in recent years, *"It is ironic that the real threat to our Democracy is the Democratic Party."* As a former Democrat, myself, I find the similarities to be shocking and I am surprised that more current Democrats do not feel the same way and do not push back on their party's current extreme, liberal, godless agenda and that lacks in common sense threatens our way of life.

Today, they are even bolder and don't even try to hide their similarities. Here is the CPUSA's message on their website in 2024:

CPUSA.org may have changed their logo, but their priorities are the same and sound even more like those of the Democratic Party that also uses noble sounding goals to protect "people and the planet" to push their climate change legislation and regulations. What also often goes unnoticed is that Democrats often claim to be the party of science to enhance their credibility with initiatives like climate change (that cannot be quantifiably proven or disproven) but conveniently avoid that claim, along with truth in general, when discussing things like abortion, the number of genders that God created, or when trying to justify that males should compete in female sports or use their bathrooms.

Are these all coincidences?

The similarities between the Communist and Democratic parties could all be a coincidence. So could the fact that the Communist Party USA was founded in Chicago (in 1919), one of the most liberal, left leaning cities in the country. It could also be a coincidence that the president who got socialized medicine (one of their primary goals) implemented in America, under the guise of "The Affordable Care Act", was President Barrack Obama who also came out of Chicago?

It could also be a coincidence that the Communist Party USA moved their headquarters to New York (and rumored to have offices in DC) around the same time that Barack Obama and his wife bought a home in the middle of Washington D.C., then another one in Cape Cod, Massachusetts?

At a minimum, these coincidences should be concerning to all of us.

Another vast array of coincidences occurred to me after listening to talks by Dr. Ben Carson, a retired neurosurgeon, the 17th U.S. Secretary of Housing and Urban Development, and a former U.S. Presidential Candidate. In them, he explains the shocking degree to which many of the Communist's goals have already been achieved in the United States.

Unbeknownst to me, Dr. Carson has been vigorously warning us since at least 2014 (when he appeared on Fox News) about Communism and what the progressives are trying to do to the American family and what they are trying to do to destroy our Judeo-Christian values and morality.

In a more recent speech at the Faith & Freedom Coalition Conference held at the Washington Hilton in June 2024, Dr. Carson asked the crowd:

"Do you know why they want to fundamentally change us?

It's because the United States of America is the major obstacle to One World Government. They cannot bring us down militarily, so what do you do next? You go inside. You divide the people on the basis of race, age, income, gender, religion, political affiliation."

Here is a list of the 45 Goals of Communism in America he spotlighted and that have already been accomplished:

- Gain control of the public schools and the teachers' union to indoctrinate the kids.
- Gain control of the news media and Hollywood so you can manipulate opinions of the people.

- Remove God from the public square.
- Go into the churches and change the real Gospel for the Social Gospel.
- Diminish the role of the family.
- Drive wedges between parents and their children.
- Make sexual perversion normal, natural and healthy.

True to form, though, I wanted to confirm what he was talking about before repeating it. (This reminds me of Ronald Reagan's mantra: "Trust but verify.") So, I ordered a copy of the book that he continually references. It's called *The Naked Communist* by W. Cleon Skousen. Here are some excerpts from Chapter 13: The 45 GOALS OF COMMUNISM TODAY.

"The 45 Goals of Communism were first published in the 8th edition of *The Naked Communist* in March 1961. They were gleaned from testimony given to Congress by various scholars and from the writings of current and former Communists. In 1963, these 45 goals were read into the Congressional Record by Albert S. Herlong, Jr. (D-Florida) and have since been shared world-wide.

The general thrust of the 45 goals was to attack the Judeo-Christian underpinning that had long prospered and protected freedom, and to replace them with the bricks, mortar, and top-down force of a purely socialistic society. Despite the fact that no such utopian society as pure socialism is possible, and that all prior attempts have destroyed civilizations for ages past, the Communists and their supporters put forward the same formula anyway. The goal, after all, was not to advance human welfare, but to advance human control."

Here are a few more that that caught my attention and have largely been accomplished:

- (#13) Do away with all loyalty oaths.

- (#15) Capture one or both of the political parties.
- (#17) Get control of the schools. Use them as transmission belts for socialism and current Communist propaganda. Put the party line in textbooks.
- (#19) Uses student protests to foment public protests.
- (#20) Infiltrate the press.
- (#21) Gain control of key positions in radio, TV and pictures.
- (#25) Break down cultural standards of morality by promoting pornography and obscenity in books, magazines, motion pictures, radio and TV.
- (#26) Present homosexuality, degeneracy and promiscuity as "normal, natural and healthy."
- (#27) Infiltrate the churches and replace revealed religion with "social" religion.
- (#28) Eliminate prayer or any phase of religious expression in the schools on the

grounds that it violates the principle of "separation of church and state."

- (#29) Discredit the American Constitution and our Founding Fathers.
- (#30) Discredit the American Founding Fathers.
- (#31) Belittle all forms of American culture and discourage the teaching of American history.
- (#32) Support any socialistic movement to give centralized control over any part of the culture.
- (#37) Infiltrate and gain control of big business.
- (#40) Discredit the family as an institution. Encourage promiscuity and easy divorce

Prior to hearing Dr. Ben Carson talk about them, I had never heard of the 45 Goals of Communism. I am hoping it was all part of God's plans to delay the publishing of this book so that I was able to include sound bites from his talks to help wake up America.

What's especially strange about this is that when the Cold War ended, I had the sinking feeling that the Communists were going underground. And history seems to have proven it.

Do all these "coincidences" surprise you? They would surprise me, too, if it wasn't for a chance encounter that I had in Oklahoma City with a Communist Cowboy in 2012! It was during my 50 Capitols in 50 Days trip as I was about to walk into the famous Cattleman's Café that I saw this rugged looking cowboy complete with the hat, boots, coat and wearing one yellowish glove that I thought was rubber.

He was so distinctive and such an anomaly that I asked to take a picture with him. After he asked where I was from and I told him "Chicago", he said, "I haven't been there since

1984 when I attended the Communist Convention."

I was speechless. Groping for something to say and distract him from the shocked look on my face, I replied, "I'm glad you've seen the light." He said, "I haven't. Now I'm a Democratic Socialist." Our conversation didn't last much longer.

Up until then, I never knew about the existence of the Communist Party USA...or that its roots were in Chicago. Oh, how I wish that this book will be read by millions of liberals and Democrats so they can better understand what is happening to America and do something about it!

Sometimes we can be inspired and learn the most about these trends from the very people who moved here from other countries to get away from those forms of government. Why? Some immigrants come to America seeking religious freedom, similarly to our founding fathers. Others come here simply for a better opportunity. But many, if not most of them, lived under similar socialistic, atheistic and communistic policies that threatened their freedoms and that we now see creeping into America.

The next chapter contains interviews of just a few of the immigrants who were coincidentally and providentially brought into my life to share their stories about the consequences of not standing up.

Chapter 10
Through the Eyes of Immigrants

Fr. Theodore (born in Kuwait)

"The America we see in the world is the Hollywood version of it, which isn't the real America that is a bit more pious and a little more God fearing. People here are more openly religious, especially when I got here, and I liked that you could be more unabashedly religious.

"Though many people today are more antagonistic about religion and faith. In Kuwait back in the 1980's, you were not allowed to say Christmas or Bible and now I come to America – the Land of the Free – and we're not allowed to say certain words in a public context but for a different reason. I find that ironic.

"We grew up in the Middle East as a minority and understand why sometimes people would try to neglect our presence by forcing the idea of the majority on us. the government should not favor one religion over another. Today, the problem is that in the schools, there is a specific ideology under the pretext of separation of church and state. The idea has to be about freedom and be an even playing field, not to favor one ideology over another.

"Today, the biggest problem is in the schools. We are being faced with the reality that our children are being bombarded with a moral reality that we never expected to find our children. So now, we are almost in our own ghetto like in Egypt within our own churches and putting our kids in our own schools and Sunday School program, like the enclosed community we left, because we don't want to be confronted with issues or want our kids exposed to things morally that we're seeing in the wider community here. Some of the parents have told me, 'Father, I grew up here and I don't know if know what to tell my kids about high school now because it's different from the way I grew up here.'

I think now schools are the biggest things we are all worried about. If we're paying the taxes for schools, why not allow us to have a voucher to put them in the school of our choice?"

The following quote from a young woman born near Russia and Ukraine that echoed the concerns of the priest from the Middle East.

Veronica Braila (born in Pridnestrovia)

"When I watched movies about America, everything was new, and it seemed like the whole world was watching. And when I learned about America's motto – In God we trust – I thought, 'What motto could be more powerful than this where the whole country has this motto politically and economically.' I knew that I wanted to come see it.

"I came here and fell in love, stayed and started my family here. But unfortunately, we're turning our back on God these days, and politically, the country is going downhill. The spread of evilness is scary, and I hope and pray the trend changes."

The following observations came from a great conversation that I had with someone who describes himself as "an average American" but who certainly has an international perspective.

Ramy Shenouda (born in Egypt)

"I'm just an average guy, a Coptic, Orthodox Christian from Egypt. I do construction and build homes and am a just an average hard-working American. My parents came here for freedom and opportunity.

"This is the greatest country in the world, and everyone has the chance to become more successful than where they came from.

"When we watched movies about this country, we saw a lot of things on TV and western movies with families even praying before dinner, for example. This country had very high moral values and there was a big focus on family structure. And that was all something to be very proud of.

But these days, all that is good is heading in the wrong direction. The country has turned away from God and pushing a very bad agenda that is against everything that we believe in. We believe in God, family structure and hard work, but this is not what we are seeing today. We are seeing false propaganda.

We are seeing the glorification of homosexuality and pedophilia, and these are just things that are just unacceptable to most immigrants.

"I think Christians are being targeted today and persecuted, which is really a shock because one of the reasons why a lot of people came to this country is freedom of religion.

"Right now, Christianity is being demonized, while homosexuality and pedophilia are being glorified. Everything today is really upside down and I think this is a terrible thing to happen in this country. This is being promoted by the greatest threat to this country and that is Democrats and corrupt politicians on both sides.

"I am still optimistic, however, and believe we will make it through this, and that this is a very temporary period. I think people have been brainwashed by false propaganda all day long, like CNN, but people are starting to wake up and they are realizing that they have been deceived."

The following comments came from another providential conversation I had with the owner of, you guessed it, a barbershop. He was born in America but spent a lot of time in Mexico. He's a young man, but an old soul who has a very mature view of what he just saw in our school system and what worries him about America.

Alonso G. (Mexican heritage)

"I was mainly raised by my mom, but my dad was around and had another family. I had to figure things out very young since the area that I grew up in was not the best and I was put in situations that forced me to grow up quickly. I think for sure the opportunities in this country are great and an improvement in terms of me and my family compared to how

102

my parents grew up.

"What worries me most is how divided we have become and the increase in violence. Where I grew up in a more impoverished area, there was violence, but it was amongst groups who had their own internal conflicts. But now there are carjackings in random places and violence where typically you were safe. As I got older and went away to school in suburban Indiana, but when I came back to some of the areas that I used to hang out at (to get away from the drama), it was not the best anymore.

"I also feel like there's a push to be open to a lot of people's beliefs, but it's almost like bit of a hypocrisy because those same people are turning down those who have other beliefs, or more conservative beliefs and accusing us, saying, "You're wrong, immoral or evil." When they are the ones who are being totally intolerant of anyone who is moral or a belief in God. If you're willing to push your rights and your beliefs, you should be tolerant of others promoting their beliefs as well, and I don't see that happening.

"This was true especially in higher education where I was being forced to close my mouth in a lot of situations. Maybe there were things that I didn't agree with, but if you speak up you're made out be like a criminal and get yelled at while in college. It is like indoctrination. Their narrative is that religion tries to indoctrinate people, but I was being indoctrinated. One of the beauties of the country is to be able to have your own opinion and beliefs. For one, I'm spending a lot of money and it's supposed to help shape my future, and I'm told what to think...and I wasn't a fan of that. I wasn't cool with being told my family's beliefs were wrong.

"God is also being pushed out of our lives in this country, while my relatives in Mexico have stood more intact with their faith. It's definitely being pushed out and we're hearing things like, 'Oh, you're one of them!' In a way, they've created a religion of their own called a 'Non-religion.'

"I just think that hypocrisy is one of my biggest issues. If you want to push something, don't be against someone else expressing their views."

Mister C. (Born in China)

This gentleman chose to remain anonymous and so I will just refer to him as Mister C. He is the Chinese guy (for lack of a better description) that I mentioned earlier, and his quote is worth repeating, so here it is again: *America is looking more and more like China these days, and unless you white guys start standing up, we're screwed.*

Mister C's quote, enthusiasm and

conviction was so infectious, he inspired the title of this book, and even its writing. I was hoping he would not want to be anonymous, but I understand and respect his wishes. He has so much wisdom and insight to share and here are couple exact quotes that he literally texted me as I was typing this paragraph:

"I would encourage all white kids to learn from their parents about their ancestors who built the wonders of Western civilization. Honor your ancestors with pride."

Plus, this one: "They are not hiding anymore; the enemies are within who don't allow you to criticize them. "

The number of random conversations that I have had with immigrants concerned with the direction of our country have been countless. I wish that I could recall and interview all of them. Some of them still echo in my ears. Here are a few of them:

- The limo driver in Florida, Alex, originally from Russia, who told my wife and I about what happened to his grandparents after the communists took over his country. His grandfather was a very successful farmer and breeder of horses and was approached by officials that they wanted to take over his business. He refused. So, one day, soldiers knocked on his front door to make their demands in person and he refused again. Then, one by one, the soldiers shot the horses and took over the business, his land, money, and possessions by force.

- My friend Paul, who grew up in Communist Poland, who expressed his concerns about the double standards we see in politics and our two-tier justice system, our uncontrolled deficit, inflation and the overreach of the federal government. He fears a potential civil war if things don't turn around.

- An Egyptian gentleman, Refaat, who told me about his disappointment in America so emphatically, that I can still picture in his eyes when he exclaimed, "This is not the country that I move here to sixty years ago!"

- The three women from Idaho who I met at the Denver State Capitol that were going to every state capitol over a three year period to pray that America would start allowing Jesus back in our lives once again.

- And, my friend, Rich, whose Italian father used to constantly warn him about the perils of our children being indoctrinated in our public schools and the threats to our democracy if people only voted on emotions and were not well educated on the merits of candidates or the issues.

This is just a small sampling of immigrants and others who certainly opened my eyes up to things that either I didn't know about or that just didn't hurt bad enough to do anything about it. They gave me the courage to stand up and, for that, I am eternally grateful and wanted to share some of their stories to encourage others to do the same.

On a more positive note, there is another immigrant, too, who I met several years ago and have admired for similar reasons. Nick Adams moved from Australia to America to get away from the things he didn't like happening in his country and to promote the American values that he felt were slipping away in America. Working as a motivational speaker and conservative activist, Nick has been tirelessly promoting love for our country and its founding principles since his first speech on American soil. I would know...since we sponsored it in Illinois.

Nick is a frequent guest on Fox News and similar media channels, and even founded a non-profit Foundation for Liberty and American Greatness (F.L.A.G.) to promote American exceptionalism in schools.

Chapter 11
How to STAND UP

There isn't enough room to completely cover this topic either, and not the purpose of this book, but this chapter contains some ideas on things you can do to STAND UP for truth and excellence and the principles upon which our country was built.

I would suggest to start by re-reading the Declaration of Independence with special emphasis on "We hold these Truths to be self-evident, that all Men are created equal, that they are endowed by our Creator with certain inalienable rights". Then, read the Gettysburg Address and memorize these words: "We here highly resolve that these dead shall not have died in vain" and "that government of the people, by the people, for the people shall not perish from the earth."

Please also pay close attention, and take an honest look, at how our country has changed over the last one hundred years. This battle has been going on since at least that, which really came to my attention when I met the great, great granddaughter of Harry Atwood. He wrote the book *Keep God in American History* back in 1919 to counter what was happening even back in Woodrow Wilson's presidency. And, more recently, compare today's sentiment to the days when President John F. Kennedy inspired unity and personal responsibility with his profound, patriotic words:

> My fellow Americans, ask not what your country can do for you, ask what you can do for your country.
>
> John F. Kennedy
> 35th U.S. President

His proclamation and way of thinking is a thing of the past and is not how socialism works. Oh, how I wish that the Democrats would also internalize the words in one of JFK's other famous quotes:

"Let every nation know, whether it wishes us well or ill, that we shall pay the price, bear any burden, meet any hardship, support any friend, oppose any foe, to assure the survival and success of liberty."

Next, look closely at what your children, nephews, nieces, and grandchildren are being taught in school. Get involved and attend school board or municipal meetings and run for public office if you need to.

Plus, be sure to exercise one thing that too many people ignore but is one of the fundamental rights of every American: Vote. And vote with your wallet by supporting the companies that support your values,

American ideals, biblical principles, and those who will both preserve our country and help it forever be, as Abraham Lincoln said, "The last, best hope on Earth."

You may also want to get involved in your children's school, be willing to voice your opinion and call out things that are not healthy or follow common sense. Another way to stand up is to get involved with your church or join a service club like the Rotary, Lions Club, Kiwanis or the Knights of Columbus. Don't assume anything and leave everything up to someone else to do all the work and pay the price.

Emulate/Support Role Models

Do you know of anyone, personally or via social media, whom you really admire what and how they are preserving the American Dream and way of life? If you do, try to do what they do, or support them in continuing their work. If the former, I understand. You may not have the time, inclination, skills, or because that is just not a strength you want to develop. I get it. There's only so much time in the day and we all have to play to our own strengths and use the gifts that God has given us to the best of our ability. Earning an income may also be a factor.

If you can't think of anyone that you admire for "standing up" for their faith and patriotism in the workplace, neighborhood, public schools, or someone trying to defend the principles upon which our country was founded in the public sector or elsewhere, here are a few of my favorite patriots and believers that you may want to follow and/or support. I have met most of them, know some personally, admire all and others from afar in alphabetical order:

- Nick Adams (Best-selling Author, Presidential Appointee, Founder of

F.L.A.G.)

- Adam Andrzejewski (President, OpenTheBooks.com, - in Memoriam)
- Ben Carson (Retired Neurosurgeon, Academic, Former HUD Secretary)
- Lauren Daigle (Christian Singer)
- Riley Gaines (12-time NCAA All-American Swimmer, Advocate, Author)
- David Green (CEO, Hobby Lobby and Founder of the Bible Museum)
- Jeannie Ives (Political Activist/Former Illinois State Representative)
- Charlie Kirk (Conservative Political Activist, Author, Radio Talk Show Host)
- Fr. Thomas Koys (Pastor, Author, Pro-Life Advocate, Radio Show Host)
- Sara Kroger (Catholic Worship Leader Songwriter and Singer)
- Candace Owens (Conservative Commentator, Author, Media Personality)
- Dan Proft (Commentator,

Entrepreneur, Lawyer, and Political Activist)
- Vivek Ramaswamy (Entrepreneur, Former U.S. Presidential Candidate)
- Mark Robinson (Lieutenant Governor of North Carolina, Black Conservative)
- Tom Selleck (American Actor, Devout Christian)
- Ben Shapiro (Syndicated Columnist, Political Pundit, Lawyer, Author)
- Toni Stockton (Mother of four, Homeschool Educator, Advocate, Writer, follower of Jesus)
- _____
- _____
- _____
- _____
- _____
- _____

(Feel free to add a few of your own.)

Mickey Straub

Sometimes the most compelling stories come from fellow parents and everyday Americans who had the courage to stand up and take action in real life so we can learn from what they went through.

The final story is an excerpt of real-life occurrences from a mom, friend, and colleague who saw what was happening in her church and children's school inside the Beltway, in a prominent suburb of Washington D.C.

Suzanne Carawan and her family stood up and her story can inspire any person of deep faith, especially my fellow Catholics and Christians. And, hopefully my many Muslim, Jewish and Hindu friends will be equally inspired to do the same.

Chapter 12
A Real-life Story
by Suzanne Carawan

Little did I know that we were living literally surrounded by a growing evil that was dripping on us each day through the school system, church, and social media.

Perhaps you have heard of where we lived at the time as it has been the subject of many news stories in the last few years---Loudoun County, Virginia. Yes, we lived in one of the most affluent areas of the country which included both a liberal elite urban area and very conservative rural areas. We lived on the very outskirts of the urban diaspora while dipping our toe into the rural communities with roots. The schools were known to be phenomenal and in fact, the elementary school was brand new. My oldest son was part of the first graduating class of Kenneth W. Culbert

Elementary. It was an idyllic town—there was an ice cream shop in summer, we had our own youth football field, our own little league field, multiple churches, Patrick Henry College, and access to dozens of vineyards within 10 miles of our home. It was beautiful, it was charming, and it was under attack even then.

It's only now that I can look back over the years and see how the liberal agenda was dripped onto us slowly and ---intentionally. While we stuck with the Episcopal church for a time period, we started to see how left the church was leaning and noticed older people leaving. While the public school had great teachers, we started to notice that the curriculum was introducing concepts that made me uncomfortable, and we experienced a similar trend at our church. While we were not allowed to hold a competitive field day, we were encouraged to talk to our children about "alternative types of families".

In fact, one day my oldest came home from school, ran into the house, and burst into tears in my arms. After admonishing him for leaving his little brother, I asked what was wrong. He could barely get out the words but in agony told me that it was the worst day of his life. He had learned that Santa wasn't real, and that homosexuality was a "bona fide lifestyle choice" and then was taught what homosexuality was and how it worked.

My son was in third grade. He also couldn't decide which lesson was worse but knew that both were facts that he could never unlearn or unhear.

I was reeling. My son didn't know how heterosexual sex worked, much less homosexuality. He was utterly confused, and my heart broke having to answer all of these questions while still fielding questions about

Santa, his existence, and now, Santa's sexual orientation. It was a little bit too much for me. It was this combination of events that told me that it was time to stand up.

I started to question, and I started to take action. To be honest, if I had had a close family or friends at that time, I probably would not have had the courage to stand up. The normative pressure in places like Loudoun County is so great that to stand up outs you as a social undesirable at worst and a cantankerous, bitter woman at best. The pressure is to get along to go along, the pressure is to not say anything, the pressure is to applaud those that uphold the current styles and is so intense that I knew something drastic was needed. My goal was not to save society, but to raise a strong family of men and reset a generation. Regardless of the weaponization of kindness, of girl power, and the popularity of diminishing boys and their space, I was compelled to stand up and make a change for my family.

I think it was important to give you some context of how much it took for me to stand up and still...how long it took. The courage to do it, and the trajectory that we put ourselves on ever since, was not my doing and it included moving from Virginia to Ohio, changing our church, as well as our religion, dinners, sports, finances, investments and more!

There is no way that I could have done what we've done without Him. I am but a witness and proof that when you stand up aligned to the Ten Commandments and Constitution, good things happen.

I now attend regular Bible studies and have worked up enough courage to talk to people about my conversion if asked. Writing down my story here is my next step in faith to go and spread the word to others because if I can do these ten things, anyone can. I am neither a goodie two shoes nor an ultra-disciplined all-or-nothing type of person, but far more of a sinner that understands Jesus came for people like me who live in a world in which they are constantly bombarded with temptation, stimulation, and subjugation to a society that is increasingly devoid of the principles laid out by our founding fathers that would set our nation apart from those ruled by tyranny.

To wrap up my story is to say it continues — and for that I am most blessed and grateful. Our families' decision to stand up many years ago now shines bright in my sons who are young men and going out in the world to forge their own path.

We live in the greatest country on earth where you have the power to choose your path because the Constitution gives us life, liberty, and the pursuit of freedom. May all of you be blessed with the courage and conviction that our founders had in blazing the trail for a new democratic, yet still faith-filled, approach to citizenship and fellowship.

Chapter 13
God's Call to Excellence

There are times when you and I may feel unworthy of God's call to excellence. We may possess doubts of our abilities to do "excellence" for God. Even Moses felt he didn't have the capacity to speak well, but God used him excellently to accomplish His will as long as Moses obeyed.

We have responsibilities God calls us to accomplish for Him. Often, we are "pastor/shepherds" to those we touch, especially to those we lead. People look at us as peacemakers who are doing God's work. This is what Glen observed and wrote regarding me:

"That is why you became mayor of your town, traveled to 50 Capitols in 50 days, and it's why you are a big fan of Abraham Lincoln, who 'pastored' America with inspiration and guidance in the country's most crucial era, the Civil War."

In the truest definition, a pastor is a shepherd who leads by example. Shepherds communicate to their sheep, their flocks, using their voice alone. Of course, the sheep have to listen!

We are like sheep, and as sheep, we are to listen and receive the shepherd's truth. Then, we must "think about these things" that we've heard. This becomes our prelude to the actions following the model of the shepherd.

Will all of us sometimes fail or not perform as "excellently" as we would like to? Sure. But we can all pick ourselves up and keep trying in our pursuit of perfection and heaven.

Determining "excellence" can be subjective and based on opinions and preferences unless strict, uniform measurement procedures are in place with no variations. But "Truth" is an absolute; either something is true or it's not.

So, what is truth, real truth? Truth is listed in Philippians 4:8 *first* in a lineup of important and vital characteristics of living according to the pattern established by Christ.

Who does this concern? Well, the "audience" for this book is everyone who cares enough to dare to speak, act, believe, and showcase truth and excellence in their personal life and in front of God and others.

Jesus set the standard for us when it came to truth. In John 8:31 and 32 Jesus said to the Jews who had believed him, "If you abide in my word, you are truly my disciples, [32] and you will know the truth, and the truth will set you free." And in John 18:37, Jesus told Pilate: "The reason I was born and came into the world is to testify to the truth. Everyone on the side of truth listens to me."

It's Time to STAND UP!

It's time to get mad, and it's time to stand up for truth and excellence!

It's time for America to turn back to God, instead of turning their backs on God.

It's time to think differently than society and the mainstream media is telling us to.

It's time for all Americans to stand up, and not just the white guys! It is time for every white, black, brown, and yellow American -- no matter what ethnic background, color, or creed -- to stand up as one like our nation's first motto hinted for us to do. It was first featured on the 1776 design of the Great Seal of the United States)

E Pluribus Unum
(Out of Many, One.)

It's time to "Think about whatever is true ... and excellent" as the Apostle Paul directed us.

It's time for all teachers and all government and private industry employees to stand up!

It's time for any entrepreneur and every American factory worker, farmer, policeman, fireman, pilot, salesperson, athlete, doctor, nurse, barista, store clerk, bagger and computer programmer to stand up!

It's time for all those who want to spread love for God and country - and unify Americans once again – to Stand up!

It's time for every Democrat, Republican, Libertarian and Independent, to Stand up for Truth and Excellence in America ...

... as if our future and possessions, the

sovereignty of our nation and eternal life, depend on it?

They do.

It's Time to STAND UP!

Mickey Straub

Acknowledgments

I am grateful that Glen Aubrey, a musician, Emmy Award Winner, publisher, and author of a dozen books himself, for planting the seed by being so persistent, and getting the ball rolling for this book. Many of his books were about Lincoln, who was the "link" that connected us. No pun intended. Abraham Lincoln was the president who kept our nation united through our greatest time of peril and whom I also credit and thank for fueling my love for God and country enough to make this book possible and for the energy to keep his vital and timeless message alive.

The number of people who have inspired me directly and indirectly to write this book, and continue to spread love for God and country, are so numerous it would take up all these pages and then some to list them all and I am sure some would be missed. Thank you! I

132

owe you all my endless gratitude for my faith and patriotism.

But there are a few people who directly contributed to this book that I would like to acknowledge, spotlight and show my appreciation, especially to Suzanne Carawan, my contributing author. Her story, of faith, patriotism, courage and love for family and country are boundless, and should inspire us all. (Thank you also for helping me become a better writer!)

To acknowledge the people who I interviewed and quoted in this book would only begin to show my appreciation for their contributions and inspiration. Special thanks go to Fr. Theodore, Veronica Braila, Paul P., Ramy Shenouda and Alonso G. who are already standing up in their own lives and are now joining me to inspire you.

And, of course, I need to thank the Chinese

gentleman who, providentially inspired me to write this book, as well as unknowingly provided the title. He chose to remain anonymous for now, but you'll be reading and learning more about his story and advice later.

Additional thanks go to that late Garry Kinder and Jack Kinder, devout Christians and true patriots, who were the first businessmen that I ever met who prayed before eating lunch and who introduced me to Roaring Lambs a couple of decades ago. That connection would eventually lead to being reintroduced to Donna Skell, Executive Director at Roaring Lambs and Marji Laine, Director of Roaring Lambs Publishing. Thank you for helping me help America stand up! (And a shout out to Mary Ann Davis for connecting us again!)

I would also like to thank Tamara Dever for the outstanding cover design (and who edited my first book) and Chastity Vasco for creating and donating the cover photo.

Thank you also to my fellow Knights of Columbus members and Father Thomas Koys and Padraic O'Connor from my former parish family at St. James at Sag Bridge who had a direct impact on this book. That church not only has parishioners it has evangelists, all of whom earned a shout out and my perpetual gratitude for firing up my faith and patriotism.

And special thanks to my wife, daughter, son-in-law, siblings and extended family who inspire me every day, and put up with my sometimes-zealous nature while looking past my many shortcomings. God bless and love to you all!

About the Author

Born and raised in northeastern Pennsylvania (Wilkes-Barre and Kingston) and the youngest of six children, Mickey Straub started his working career early, in grade school, working at a pool hall then a paper route, and working at Hess gas station in high school and college for former Marine, Joe Mantione.

After graduating from Indiana University of Pennsylvania where he majored in Criminology and minored in Political Science, he moved to Washington D.C. and started with the Department of Interior for a few months, until an investigative job opened-up at the U.S. Department of Defense (DOD). As he has told audiences for years, "I was an agent for 16 years: 2 years as a federal agent and 14 years as an insurance agent. As a federal investigator, he was transferred to Los Angeles for a couple years. DOD is where his patriotism grew immensely, but also where he became disappointed by the work ethic of federal employees and exposed to the reality and negative consequences of the multiple public pension system. He went to work for a Chicago based insurance company, where he moved a few years later, initially for Pat Ryan & Associates, then Western Diversified, a subsidiary of John Alden Life Insurance. He spent the bulk of his career in the Chicagoland area.

Mickey is CEO and founder of SAMUSA,

Inc., formerly known as Sales Activity Management, a company and industry he founded in 1995 to "empower success and make a difference" in the careers of agents and financial advisors and the managers who lead them. In an effort to support the financial services industry, Mickey also served on the NAIFA Chicago (National Association of Insurance & Financial Advisors) board for ten years and was chairman of their legislative committee, and also was GAMA International's (now called Finseca), largest sponsor for ten years. His company is now an official partner of NAIFA and in recent years, that has brought him back to where his career started and his patriotism grew in Washington D.C. where he has also assisted in their lobbying efforts to protect the financial services industry and their clients.

SAMUSA is a patriotic, faith-based company that provides success management tools and services across the financial services profession and other industries to help them achieve their goals. Goal setting was a skill he developed early, whether it was playing pool competitively, cycling or buying and selling cars all at an early age. He owned 13 cars before graduating college and 76 since then, and his goal is to reach 100. His passion for striving for goals, and helping others do the same, continues.

His first foray into politics was when he founded Proud to be Republican, LLC, a campaign services company that supported principled Republicans across Illinois. He was elected (twice) as Mayor of Burr Ridge, Illinois, a prominent Chicago suburb, where Mickey also served on the veterans memorial committee for twelve years, four as chairman. Nicknamed "Mayor Mickey," he has been married for thirty-nine years to Charmaine and they have one daughter, Alysa. Mickey is a keynote speaker, Knights of Columbus member, and a devout Catholic who recently created a brochure called

Mickey Straub

The Four Levels of the Rosary for the Easily Distracted.

Mickey is also the author of *BIG Goals…Short Deadlines*, an inspirational book with a patriotic and spiritual message. In it, he outlines the five Habits of Success for overcoming adversity and achieving personal and professional goals, while using his 50 Capitols in 50 Days trip in honor of Abraham Lincoln and our veterans to illustrate them. That patriotic pilgrimage also earned him a Congressional Record from the U.S. House of Representatives.

He now resides in Hendersonville, Tennessee, a Nashville suburb, where his mission continues, "To spread love for God and country", which is ultimately the goal of this book. Besides politics, taxes and weather, he moved to Tennessee to write more patriotic, faith-based books and to form a 501(c)(3) organization called the 50 Capitols Foundation.

It's Time to Stand Up

Mickey Straub

About the Contributing Author

Suzanne Carawan grew up in the Washington, D.C. area. Confirmed at the Washington National Cathedral following in the footsteps of her mother's family, Suzanne was a Protestant for nearly 40 years before converting to Catholicism. Starting at Ohio State University, Suzanne transferred to the University of Maryland, College Park as her mother was a case study of esophageal cancer and seeking treatment at Georgetown University. Following her death, Suzanne stayed in the D.C. area at the request of her father.

Following graduation, Suzanne moved to Atlanta and then went on to study at Columbia University and Tulane University over the next few years. She returned to the D.C. area to work in consulting, and it was in Bethesda, Maryland that she eventually met and married her husband, John. She earned her MBA from American University at night, graduating four months pregnant. This set the pace of their married life as they welcomed in two sons, Jackson and Blake, who have taken the family on an incredible number of faith-filled journeys through their sports and hobbies. Before the boys began middle school, the family picked-up and moved to Columbus, Ohio to allow them to live according to their values and faith.

(To read Suzanne's complete story, visit www.50CapitolsFoundation.org.)

America is at a precipice and a turning point, and the only way we are going to … "highly resolve" and to spark that "new birth of freedom", so that "a government of the people, by the people, for the people, shall not perish from the earth"

… is to Stand Up!

But please remember, this is not just about one election, president or Congress. It's a marathon, not a sprint.

It's Time to

Stand Up

for Truth and Excellence

. . . in America!

www.ingramcontent.com/pod-product-compliance
Lightning Source LLC
Chambersburg PA
CBHW060904280326
41934CB00007B/1173